漂鸟集
Stray Birds

泰戈尔 - 著
Rabindranath Tagore works

伍晴文 - 译
Wu qingwen Translator

文匯出版社

图书在版编目（CIP）数据

漂鸟集 /（印）泰戈尔著；伍晴文译. -- 上海：文汇出版社，2016.5
ISBN 978-7-5496-1702-9

Ⅰ.①漂… Ⅱ.①泰… ②伍… Ⅲ.①诗集—印度—现代 Ⅳ.①I351.25

中国版本图书馆CIP数据核字（2016）第027706号

漂鸟集

出 版 人 / 桂国强
作　　者 / 泰戈尔
责任编辑 / 戴　铮
封面装帧 / 粉粉猫
出版发行 / 文汇出版社
　　　　　上海市威海路755号
　　　　　（邮政编码200041）
经　　销 / 全国新华书店
印刷装订 / 三河市金泰源印务有限公司
版　　次 / 2016年5月第1版
印　　次 / 2016年5月第1次印刷
开　　本 / 889×1194　1/32
字　　数 / 128千字
印　　张 / 6

ISBN 978-7-5496-1702-9
定　价：29.00元

001

夏天的漂鸟，来到我窗前歌唱，
又飞走了。
而秋天的黄叶，无歌欢唱，
轻叹一声，飘落在地。

002

喔，这群世上的小小流浪者啊，
请将你们的足迹留在我的字里行间！

001

Stray birds of summer come to my window to sing and fly away.
And yellow leaves of autumn, which have no songs,
flutter and fall there with a sigh.

002

O Troupe of little vagrants of the world,
leave your footprints in my words.

003

世界向它的爱人，卸下它巨大的面具。

它变得小如一首歌，如一个永恒之吻。

004

是大地的泪珠，

让她的微笑一直绽放着。

003

The world puts off its mask of vastness to its lover.

It becomes small as one song, as one kiss of the eternal.

004

It is the tears of the earth that

keep her smiles in bloom.

005

浩瀚的大漠，对一叶绿草燃起热烈爱火，
而她却摇了摇头，笑着飞走了。

006

你若因为错过太阳而哭蒙了眼，

那你也将错过星群。

005

The mighty desert is burning for the love of a blade of grass

who shakes her head and laughs and flies away.

006

If you shed tears when you miss the sun,

you also miss the stars.

007

舞动的流水啊,

途中的泥沙正乞求你的歌声与流动。

你是否愿意挟起不良于行的泥沙前行俱下?

007

The sands in your way beg for

your song and your movement,

dancing water.

Will you carry the burden of their lameness?

008
她热切的容颜,
宛如夜晚的雨滴,缠扰我梦。

009
我们曾梦见彼此陌路。
醒来时才发现,我们本是亲密无间。

008
Her wishful face haunts my dreams
like the rain at night.

009
Once we dreamt that we were strangers.
We wake up to find that we were dear to each other.

010
在我心中业已归于平静的忧伤,
宛如降落在寂林中的夜幕。

011
一些看不见的手指,像慵懒的微风,
在我心弦弹奏着篇篇乐章。

010
Sorrow is hushed into peace in my heart like the
evening among the silent trees.

011
Some unseen fingers, like an idle breeze,
are playing upon my heart the music of the ripples.

012

"喔,大海啊,您说的是什么话语?"
"是永恒的疑问。"
"喔,穹空啊,您的回答又是什么?"
"是永恒的沉默。"

012

"What language is thine, O Sea?"
"The language of eternal question."
"What language is thy answer, O Sky?"
"The language of eternal silence."

013
听着,我心,
听那世界的呢喃,它正在向你示爱呀。

014
造物的奥秘,
仿似夜之暗黑如许伟大。
知识却犹如晨雾般虚幻。

013
Listen, my heart, to the whispers of the world with which it makes love to you.

014
The mystery of creation is like the darkness of night — it is great.
Delusions of knowledge are like the fog of the morning.

015
莫因峭壁高耸，
而将你的爱情置之于上。

016
今天早晨，我坐在窗前，
世界宛如过客，
驻足片刻，
向我点点头便离开了。

015
Do not seat your love upon a precipice because it is high.

016
I sit at my window this morning where the world like a passer-by stops for a moment, nods to me and goes.

017

这些零碎思绪,就像树叶的簌沙声,

于我心坎细数欢乐。

018

你看不见真正的自己,

所见的只是你的影子。

017

These little thoughts are the rustle of leaves;

they have their whisper of joy in my mind.

018

What you are you do not see,

what you see is your shadow.

019

主啊,我的那些愿望真是痴傻,

在您的歌声中喧嚷着。

让我单纯地静静聆听吧!

020

我无法选择最好的,

是最好的来选择我。

019

My wishes are fools, they shout across thy songs,

my Master.Let me but listen.

020

I cannot choose the best.

The best chooses me.

021

把灯笼提在身后的人，

将影子投在自己身前。

022

我的存在本身即属永恒的惊喜，

这就是生命。

021

They throw their shadows before them who

carry their lantern on their back.

022

That I exist is

a perpetual surprise which is life.

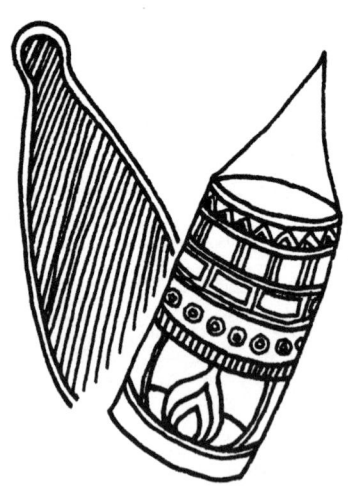

023
"我们这些沙沙作响的树叶,
　以声音响应暴风雨。
　但你是谁呀,如此沉默?"
"我只是一朵花儿。"

023
"We, the rustling leaves,
have a voice that answers the storms,
but who are you so silent?"
"I am a mere flower."

024

休息之于工作，

正如眼睑之于眼睛。

025

人好比初生的婴孩，

成长的力量即为他的力量。

024

Rest belongs to the work

as the eyelids to the eyes.

025

Man is a born child,

his power is the power of growth.

026
神期盼我们答谢,
乃是因为他送了花朵给我们,
而不是因为阳光和土地。

026
God expects answers for the flowers he sends us,
not for the sun and the earth.

027

光宛如赤子般快活地嬉游于绿叶间，
殊不知人间充斥着虚伪谎言。

028

喔，美啊，
在爱中寻找你自己，
别往镜中的阿谀里寻。

027

The light that plays, like a naked child,

among the green leaves happily knows not that man can lie.

028

O Beauty, find thyself in love,

not in the flattery of thy mirror.

029

我的心在世界的海岸拍击着她的浪花,
并以眼泪署下"我爱你"这几个字。

030

"月儿啊,你在等候什么?"
"等着问候我该让出路来的太阳。"

029

My heart beats her waves at the shore of the world and
writes upon it her signature in tears with the words,"I love thee."

030

"Moon, for what do you wait?"
"To salute the sun for whom I must make way."

031
绿叶伸长到我窗前,
宛如喑哑的大地发出渴望之声。

032
神对自己创造的清晨,
亦感到新奇无比。

031
The trees come up to my window like the
yearning voice of the dumb earth.

032
His own mornings are new surprises to God.

033

生命因对世界的索求而致富，
因对爱的索求而有了价值。

034

干涸的河床，
并不感谢它的过去。

033

Life finds its wealth by the claims of the world,

and its worth by the claims of love.

034

The dry river-bed finds no thanks for its past.

035

鸟儿愿自己是一片云。

云儿愿自己是一只鸟。

036

瀑布唱着:

"当我觅获自由时,便会找到我的歌声。"

035

The bird wishes it were a cloud.

The cloud wishes it were a bird.

036

The waterfall sings, "I find my song, when I find my freedom."

037
我不明白这心为何如此默然颓丧。
就因那些它从不问、不懂或不记得的小小需求。

037
I cannot tell why this heart languishes in silence.
It is for small needs it never asks,
or knows or remembers.

038

女人哪,

当你在料理家务四处移动时,

你的手足仿如在山涧溪流的小卵石间轻歌漫舞着。

038

Woman, when you move about

in your household service,

your limbs sing like a hill stream among its pebbles.

039

太阳横越西方之海时,
向东方留下他最后的问候。

040

别因自己没胃口而抱怨食物。

039

The sun goes to cross the Western sea,
leaving its last salutation to the East.

040

Do not blame your food because
you have no appetite.

041

树群好似大地的渴望，

踮起脚尖窥向天堂。

042

你什么也没说，仅对着我微笑，

我竟觉得这就是我等候已久的。

041

The trees, like the longings of the earth,

stand a-tiptoe to peep at the heaven.

042

You smiled and talked to me of nothing and

I felt that for this I had been waiting long.

043

水里的鱼儿是静默的,陆上的野兽是喧闹的,
空中的鸟儿是欢唱的。
可是,人却兼有大海的静默、大地的喧闹
和天上的乐音。

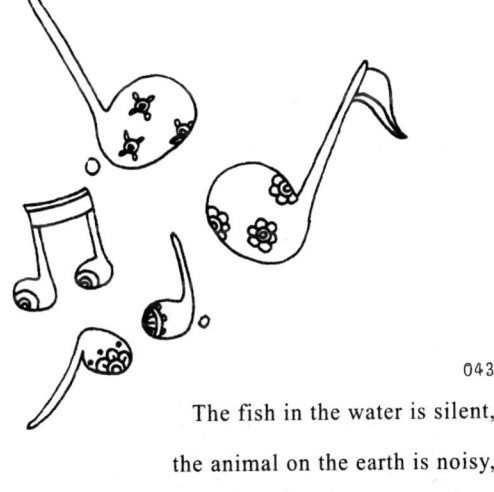

043

The fish in the water is silent,
the animal on the earth is noisy,
the bird in the air is singing.
But Man has in him the silence of the sea,
the noise of the earth and the music of the air.

044
世界滑过踌躇的心弦,
奏出忧伤的乐曲。

045
将自己的武器视为神的人,
当武器得胜时,他却被自己打败了。

044
The world rushes on over the strings of
the lingering heart making the music of sadness.

045
He has made his weapons his gods.
When his weapons win he is defeated himself.

046
神在创造中,找到自己。

047
影子戴上她的面纱,
用她静蹑的爱之脚步,
悄柔地追随着"光"。

046
God finds himself by creating.

047
Shadow, with her veil drawn,
follows Light in secret meekness,
with her silent steps of love.

048

群星不怕自己看起来像萤火虫。

049

感谢上帝，我不是那些权力之轮，
而是被它压辗而过的生灵之一。

048

The stars are not afraid to appear like fireflies.

049

I thank thee that I am none of the wheels of
power but I am one with
the living creatures that are crushed by it.

050
心智，精明但不宽阔，
执着于每个细微末节，不知前进。

051
你的偶像消散于尘土中，
证明了神的尘土比你的偶像还伟大。

050
The mind, sharp but not broad,
sticks at every point but does not move.

051
Your idol is shattered in the dust to prove that
God's dust is greater than your idol.

052

过往陈迹无法展现一个人，

唯可不断奋力向前行。

053

玻璃灯责备瓦灯擅自与之称兄道弟，

当月亮升起时，玻璃灯却殷勤笑着，

唤她："我亲爱，亲爱的姊妹。"

052

Man does not reveal himself in his history,

he struggles up through it.

053

While the glass lamp rebukes the earthen for calling it cousin,

the moon rises, and the glass lamp, with a bland smile,

calls her,—" My dear, dear sister."

054
我们就像海鸥与浪涛相遇一般,
彼此相近、相亲。
海鸥纷飞,浪涛滚滚而逝,
我们也随之分离了。

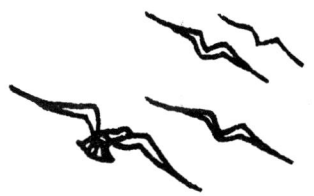

054
Like the meeting of the seagulls and the
waves we meet and come near.
The seagulls fly off,
the waves roll away and we depart.

055
一天的工作结束了,
我就像一艘被拖上岸的船只,
聆听着晚潮舞动的乐曲。

056
生命是上苍赋予的,
唯有付出生命,才算真正得到它。

055
My day is done,
and I am like a boat drawn on the beach,
listening to the dance-music of the tide in the evening.

056
Life is given to us,
we earn it by giving it.

057

我们最谦卑那刻，始最接近伟大。

058

麻雀可怜孔雀得忍受自己笨重的屏尾。

057

We come nearest to the great when we are great in humility.

058

The sparrow is sorry for the peacock at the burden of its tail.

059

永不畏惧"短暂的瞬间"

——永恒之声如此唱着。

060

飓风在绝路中寻找快捷方式,

却又在绝地倏然停止搜寻。

059

Never be afraid of the moments—thus sings the voice of the everlasting.

060

The hurricane seeks the shortest road by the no-road, and suddenly ends its search in the Nowhere.

061

就我的酒杯饮了我的酒吧,朋友。

环浮其上的泡沫一倒入别人的酒杯,

便会消失了。

062

"完美"因爱慕"不完美",

而以美来装扮自己。

061

Take my wine in my own cup, friend.

It loses its wreath of foam when poured into that of others.

062

The Perfect decks itself in beauty for the

love of the Imperfect.

063

神对人类说：

"我为了治愈你而伤害你，我因爱你而惩罚你。"

064

感谢灯焰的光明，

但也别忘了坚忍站在黑暗中的灯台啊。

063

God says to man,"I heal you therefore I hurt, love you therefore punish."

064

Thank the flame for its light, but do not forget the lampholder standing in the shade with constancy of patience.

065

小草啊，

你的脚步虽小，却拥有脚下的大地。

066

幼嫩的花朵绽放它的花蕾并喊道：

"亲爱的世界啊，请别凋谢。"

065

Tiny grass, your steps are small,

but you possess the earth under your tread.

066

The infant flower opens its bud and cries,

"Dear World, please do not fade."

067

神逐渐厌烦庞大的王国，

却永不厌倦那小小的花朵。

068

邪恶经不起考验，

正义却可以。

067

God grows weary of great kingdoms,

but never of little flowers.

068

Wrong cannot afford defeat but Right can.

069

瀑布歌唱着：

"尽管一瓢水便足以止渴，

　但我却欢欢喜喜地献出我的全部。"

069

"I give my whole water in joy,"

sings the waterfall,

"though little of it is enough for the thirsty."

070

以不断迸流进出的欢乐涌流，将这些花朵抛掷而上的那座泉源在哪儿啊？

071

樵夫的斧头向树乞求斧柄。
树便给了它。

070

Where is the fountain that throws up these flowers in a ceaseless outbreak of ecstasy?

071

The woodcutter's axe begged for its handle from the tree.
The tree gave it.

072

在我孤寂的心里,

察觉到这雾雨蒙蒙的孤独夜所发出之叹息。

073

贞洁是从丰盈之爱中滋养出来的财富。

072

In my solitude of heart I feel the sigh of

this widowed evening veiled with mist and rain.

073

Chastity is a wealth that comes from abundance of love.

074
雾，
宛如爱情，在山丘的心头上嬉戏，
引领出种种美丽的惊喜。

075
我们误解了世界，
却反控世界骗了我们。

074
The mist, like love,
plays upon the heart of the hills and
brings out surprises of beauty.

075
We read the world wrong and say that it deceives us.

076
诗人的风穿越海洋和森林，
追寻自己的声音。

077
每个孩子出生，
都带来了上帝尚未对人类失望的神谕。

076

The poet wind is out over the sea and

the forest to seek his own voice.

077

Every child comes with the message that

God is not yet discouraged of man.

078

小草在大地寻找她的伙伴。

大树往空中寻找他的孤寂。

078

The grass seeks her crowd in the earth.

The tree seeks his solitude of the sky.

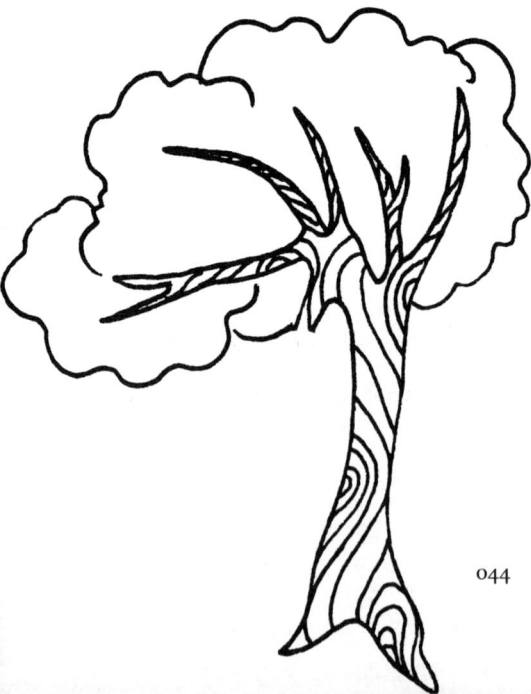

079

人类常对自己筑起堤防。

080

我的朋友,你的话音徘徊在我心中,

就像大海的低吟,

回荡在静静聆听的松林间。

079

Man barricades against himself.

080

Your voice, my friend, wanders in my heart,

like the muffled sound of the

sea among these listening pines.

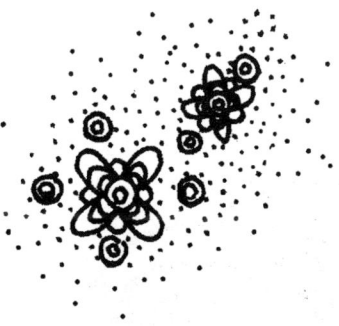

081
这黑暗中将火花化为繁星的隐形之火,
到底是什么?

082
愿生命如盛夏花朵般美灿,
死亡亦如秋天落叶般静好。

081
What is this unseen flame of darkness
whose sparks are the stars?

082
Let life be beautiful like summer flowers and
death like autumn leaves.

083
想行善的人在门口敲着门，
想献出爱的人会发现门已为之敞开。

084
众生在死中合而为一；
一在生中幻化为众生。
当神死时，宗教终将合而为一。

083
He who wants to do good knocks at the gate;
he who loves finds the gate open.

084
In death the many becomes one; in life the one becomes many.
Religion will be one when God is dead.

085
艺术家是大自然的情人,
因此他是大自然的仆人,也是她的主人。

086
"果实啊,你离我有多远呢?"
"花儿啊,我就藏在你心里。"

085
The artist is the lover of Nature,
therefore he is her slave and her master.

086
"How far are you from me, O Fruit?"
"I am hidden in your heart, O Flower."

087

这份渴念，

是那些自觉身处于黑暗中的人才感受得到，

在白昼中便无从得见。

088

露珠对湖水说：

"你是荷叶下的大露珠，

我是荷叶上的小露珠。"

087

This longing is for the one who is felt in the dark,

but not seen in the day.

088

"You are the big drop of dew under the lotus leaf,

I am the smaller one on its upper side,"

said the dewdrop to the lake.

089

刀鞘为了保护刀的锋利,

而自足于本身的驽钝。

090

在黑暗中,"一"视若一体;

在光亮中,"一"则视若众多样貌。

089

The scabbard is content to be dull when it protects the keenness of the sword.

090

In darkness the One appears as uniform;
in the light the One appears as manifold.

091

在绿草的点缀下,

大地显得宜人可居。

092

绿叶的生死如旋涡疾速转动,

而较外缘的回流,则缓行于星辰间。

091

The great earth makes herself hospitable

with the help of the grass.

092

The birth and death of

the leaves are the rapid whirls of the

eddy whose wider circles move slowly among stars.

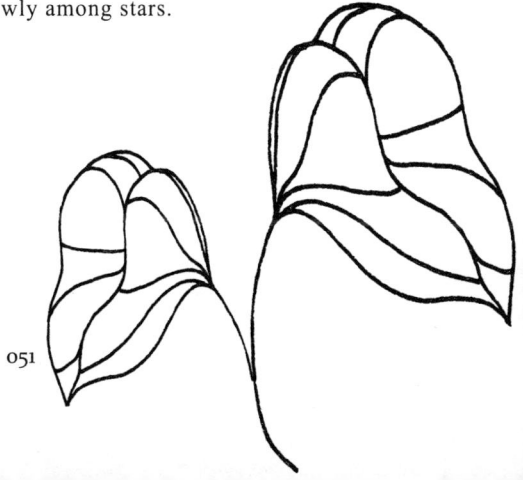

093
权力对世界说:"你是我的。"
世界遂将权力囚禁于她的宝座下。
爱对世界说:"我是您的。"
世界便给了爱出入宝殿的自由。

093
Power said to the world,"You are mine. "
The world kept it prisoner on her throne.
Love said to the world,"I am thine. "
The world gave it the freedom of her house.

094

雾宛如大地的渴望,

当大地哭求太阳时,雾便将之藏起。

095

静默吧,我心,

这些参天大树都是祈祷者呢。

094

The mist is like the earth's desire.

It hides the sun for whom she cries.

095

Be still, my heart,

these great trees are prayers.

096

短暂时刻的喧闹,

讥笑着永恒的音乐。

097

我想及那些浮沉于生命、

爱与死之流的过往岁月已遭遗忘,

于是我感知到离开尘世的自由。

096

The noise of the moment scoffs at the music of the Eternal.

097

I think of other ages that floated upon the stream of

life and love and death and are forgotten,

and I feel the freedom of passing away.

098

我灵魂的忧伤,就像新娘的面纱,

等着午夜被掀开。

099

死亡的印记赋予生命之币价值,

使其能用生命换取那些真正宝贵之物。

098

The sadness of my soul is her bride's veil.

It waits to be lifted in the night.

099

Death's stamp gives value to the coin of life;

making it possible to buy with life what is truly precious.

100

白云谦逊地站在天边一隅。

晨曦冠之以绚丽的光辉。

101

尘土饱受玷辱,却报之以花朵。

100

The cloud stood humbly in a corner of the sky.

The morning crowned it with splendour.

101

The dust receives insult and in return offers her flowers.

102

不必费心停下脚步采集花朵，

只管继续往前走，

因为花自会随着你的脚步开满路。

102

Do not linger to gather flowers to keep them,

but walk on,

for flowers will keep themselves blooming all your way.

103

根是地下的枝干。

枝干是空中的根。

104

早已远逝的夏音,飘绕着秋,

寻找它旧日的巢。

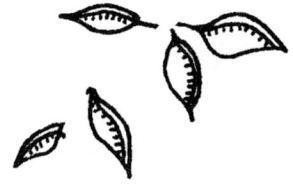

103

Roots are the branches down in the earth.

Branches are roots in the air.

104

The music of the far-away summer flutters around the

Autumn seeking its former nest.

105

别把你口袋里的功勋借给友人，

那是对他的侮辱。

106

那些无名岁月里的感触攀附我心，

宛如攀缘在老树上的青苔。

105

Do not insult your friend by lending him

merits from your own pocket.

106

The touch of the nameless days clings to my heart

like mosses round the old tree.

107

回音嘲笑她的原声,

试以证明她才是原声。

108

当飞黄腾达者吹嘘自己得到神特别的恩宠时,

神却为之羞愧。

107

The echo mocks her origin to prove she is the original.

108

God is ashamed when the prosperous boasts of

His special favour.

109

之所以将自己的影子投射在前方道路上，
乃因我还有一盏未点燃的明灯。

110

人们走入喧哗的人群，
乃为了淹没自个儿内心沉默的呐喊声。

109

I cast my own shadow upon my path,
because I have a lamp that has not been lighted.

110

Man goes into the noisy crowd to drown
his own clamour of silence.

111

枯竭的尽头是死亡,

但圆满的尽头却是永恒。

112

太阳只有一件简朴的光袍,

云朵却因此披上璀璨的衣裳。

111

That which ends in exhaustion is death,

but the perfect ending is in the endless.

112

The sun has his simple robe of light.

The clouds are decked with gorgeousness.

113
山群宛如叫跳着的孩子,高举双臂,
想要摘下星星。

114
道路在熙攘的人群间是寂寥的,
因为它不受人怜爱。

113
The hills are like shouts of children who
raise their arms, trying to catch stars.

114
The road is lonely in its crowd, for it is not loved.

115

权力吹夸着自己的恶行,

却被飘落的黄叶及路过的浮云嘲笑。

116

今天大地在阳光下对我哼唱,

宛如纺织妇,

用一种已被遗忘的语言,吟唱着古老的歌谣。

115

The power that boasts of its mischiefs is laughed at

by the yellow leaves that fall, and clouds that pass by.

116

The earth hums to me today in the sun,

like a woman at her spinning,

some ballad of the ancient time in a forgotten tongue.

117

草叶无愧于它所生长的伟大世界。

118
梦是唠叨不休的妻子。
睡眠是默默忍受的丈夫。

117

The grass-blade is worth of

the great world where it grows.

118

Dream is a wife who must talk.

Sleep is a husband who silently suffers.

119

夜吻着逐渐逝去的白昼,在他耳边低语道:

"我是死亡,你的母亲。

我将赋予你新生命。"

119

The night kisses the fading day whispering to his ear,

"I am death, your mother.

I am to give you fresh birth."

120
黑夜啊,你的美,我感觉到了,
宛似暗灯下的可爱女人。

121
我在我的世界,
扛负着促成这繁荣盛世背后的诸多失败。

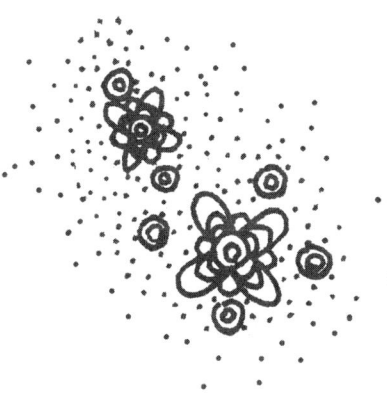

120
I feel thy beauty, dark night,
like that of the loved woman when she has put out the lamp.

121
I carry in my world that flourishes the
worlds that have failed.

122
亲爱的朋友,
每当我在海滩听着涛声时,
便感觉到你在多少暮色渐深的黄昏里,
所怀那些伟大思想的静默。

122
Dear friend, I feel the silence of your great thoughts of
many a deepening eventide on this beach when
I listen to these waves.

123

鸟以为将鱼举到空中,是一种善举。

124

黑夜对太阳说:

"你在月光下将情书送给了我,

我在草地上留下泪珠作为答复。"

123

The bird thinks it is an act of kindness to give the fish a lift in the air.

124

"In the moon thou sendest thy love letters to me," said the night to the sun.

"I leave my answers in tears upon the grass."

125
伟大是个初生的孩子；
当他死后，将他伟大的童年留给了世界。

126
不是锤子的锤炼，
而是流水的舞动——
唱得卵石臻至完美。

125
The Great is a born child;
when he dies he gives his great childhood to the world.

126
Not hammer-strokes, but dance of the water sings the pebbles into perfection.

127

蜜蜂在花丛中采蜜,
离开时嗡嗡鸣谢。
美艳的蝴蝶却理所当然认为,
花儿应向他道谢。

127

Bees sip honey from flowers and
hum their thanks when they leave.
The gaudy butterfly is sure that the
flowers owe thanks to him.

128
若你不想等待以便说出完整的真理，
逞口舌之快是很容易的。

129
"可能"向"不可能"问：
"何处是你的居所？"
"无能者的梦里。"它这么回答道。

128

To be outspoken is easy when you do not wait to
speak the complete truth.

129

Asks the Possible to the Impossible,
"Where is your dwelling-place?"
"In the dreams of the impotent,"
comes the answer.

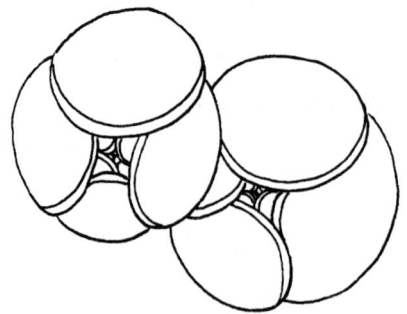

130

若你将所有的错误都关在门外，
那么就连真理也会被屏弃在外。

131

我听见有东西在我忧伤的心后沙沙作响——
可我看不见它们。

130

If you shut your door to all errors truth will be shut out.

131

I hear some rustle of things behind my sadness of heart,—
I cannot see them.

132

闲暇一旦动起来便是工作。

静止的海水一旦波动便成了浪涛。

133

叶子付出爱时,便开了花朵。

花朵崇敬神时,便成了果实。

132

Leisure in its activity is work.

The stillness of the sea stirs in waves.

133

The leaf becomes flower when it loves.

The flower becomes fruit when it worships.

134

地下的树根让树枝结出果实，
却不求回报。

135

这雨夜，风吹不息。
我望着摇曳的树枝，感念万物的伟大。

134

The roots below the earth claim no rewards for
making the branches fruitful.

135

This rainy evening the wind is restless.
I look at the swaying branches and ponder over the
greatness of all things.

136

午夜的暴风雨，

仿如不该在黑夜醒来的巨大孩子，

开始嬉戏喧闹。

137

你卷起浪涛，徒然地追随你的爱人，

啊，大海，

你这暴风雨的寂寞新娘。

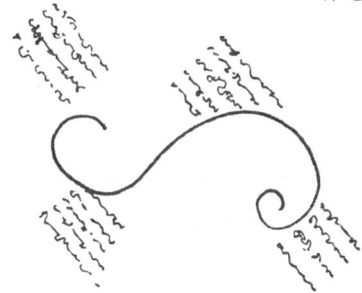

136

Storm of midnight, like a giant child awakened in

the untimely dark, has begun to play and shout.

137

Thou raisest thy waves vainly to follow thy lover,

O Sea,

thou lonely bride of the storm.

138

"我为自己的空洞感到惭愧。"

——文字对工作这般说道。

"当我看见你,便了解到自己有多贫乏。"

——工作对文字如此回话。

138

"I am ashamed of my emptiness,"

said the Word to the Work.

"I know how poor I am when I see you,"

said the Work to the Word.

139

时间是变化的宝藏,

然而时钟在它拙劣的模仿中,

只生出变化却不见宝藏。

140

"真理"穿上衣裳,却觉事实太过束缚。

在想象中,她反倒行动自如。

139

Time is the wealth of change,

but the clock in its parody makes it

mere change and no wealth.

140

Truth in her dress finds facts too tight.

In fiction she moves with ease.

141

从前我旅行到这里、那里时，

　　我厌倦了你呀，道路。

而今当你引领我走向四方时，

　　我在爱中与你结缡了。

141

When I travelled to here and to there,

I was tired of thee,

O Road,

but now when thou leadest me to everywhere

I am wedded to thee in love.

142

就让我揣想繁星中有一颗星,
引导我的生命走过那未知的黑暗吧。

143

女人,你用你优雅的手指碰触我所有之物,
秩序便如音乐般畅流而生。

142

Let me think that there is one among those stars that
guides my life through the dark unknown.

143

Woman, with the grace of
your fingers you touched my things
and order came out like music.

144

悲伤的声音在已逝年华中有个巢。

它在夜里对我唱道:"我曾爱过你。"

145

熊熊烈火用它的灼热警告我远离它。

请将我从埋在灰里的余烬中拯救出来吧!

144

One sad voice has its nest among the ruins of the years.

It sings to me in the night,—

" I loved you. "

145

The flaming fire warns me off by its own glow.

Save me from the dying embers hidden under ashes.

146
纵拥有满天的星斗,
然而,唉,我屋里的小灯却没有亮。

147
已逝的文字化为尘土粘附您身。
用静默洗涤您的灵魂吧。

146
I have my stars in the sky,
but oh for my little lamp unlit in my house.

147
The dust of the dead words clings to thee.
Wash thy soul with silence.

148

生命留下许多缺口,

死亡的哀乐从中传来。

149

世界在清晨敞开它光明的心。

出来吧,我心,

带着你的爱迎向它。

148

Gaps are left in life through

which comes the sad music of death.

149

The world has opened its heart of light in the morning.

Come out, my heart, with thy love to meet it.

150
我的思绪，随着这些闪闪发亮的叶子闪耀着；
我的心，在阳光的抚触下歌唱着；
我的生命，因得与万物同浮游于穹苍、
时间之轮里而欢喜着。

150
My thoughts shimmer with these shimmering leaves and
my heart sings with the touch of this sunlight;
my life is glad to be floating with
all things into the blue of space,
into the dark of time.

151

上帝的神威潜藏在轻柔的微风中，

而不在狂风暴雨里。

152

这只是一场梦，

梦里的所有事物分崩离析，紧紧压迫着我。

待我醒来，

我将发现所有事物均完好收放在您那里，

而我也将得到自由。

151

God's great power is in the gentle breeze, not in the storm.

152

This is a dream in which things are all loose and they oppress.

I shall find them gathered in thee when

I awake and shall be free.

153

"谁将接下我的工作？"落日问道。

"我将尽我所能，我的主人。"瓦灯应答。

154

摘下花瓣，

无法让你得到花朵的美丽。

153

"Who is there to take up my duties?" asked the setting sun.

"I shall do what I can, my Master," said the earthen lamp.

154

By plucking her petals you do not gather the beauty of the flower.

155

沉默会驮负着你的声音，

宛似鸟巢托着歇眠的鸟儿。

156

"伟大"不怕与"渺小"同行。

"平庸"却避而远之。

155

Silence will carry your voice like the nest that

holds the sleeping birds.

156

The Great walks with the Small without fear.

The Middling keeps aloof.

157

黑夜悄悄使花朵绽放,

却让白昼去接受人们的感谢。

158

"权力"视牺牲者的悲愤为忘恩负义的行为。

157

The night opens the flowers in secret and

allows the day to get thanks.

158

Power takes as ingratitude the

writhings of its victims.

159
当我们因圆满而欢喜时,
便能欣然放下我们所成就的果实。

160
雨滴亲吻着大地低语:
"我们是您思乡的孩子呀,母亲,
从天上回到您身边了。"

159
When we rejoice in our fulness,
then we can part with our fruits with joy.

160
The raindrops kissed the earth and whispered,
—"We are thy homesick children, mother,
come back to thee from the heaven."

161

蜘蛛网假装要抓住露珠,

却抓到了苍蝇。

162

爱情啊!

当你手持燃烧着痛苦的灯走来时,

我得以看见你的容颜,

并知道你就是幸福。

161

The cobweb pretends to catch

dewdrops and catches flies.

162

Love!

When you come with the burning lamp of

pain in your hand,

I can see your face and

know you as bliss.

163

"学者说你的光总有一天会消失。"

——萤火虫对星星如是说道。

星星未加回答。

163

"The learned say that

your lights will one day be no more,"

said the firefly to the stars.

The stars made no answer.

164
在黄昏暮色中,
某些拂晓之鸟来到我静默之巢。

165
思绪掠过心头,犹如飞过穹苍的一群野雁。
我听到它们鼓翼的声音。

164
In the dusk of the evening the bird of
some early dawn comes to the nest of my silence.

165
Thoughts pass in my mind like flocks of ducks in the sky.
I hear the voice of their wings.

166
运河总喜欢自认为,
河流的存在只为供应它水流。

167
世界以其苦痛亲吻我的灵魂,
竟要求我报以歌声。

166
The canal loves to think that
rivers exist solely to supply it with water.

167
The world has kissed my soul with its pain,
asking for its return in songs.

168
压迫着我的,
是我那试图挣脱而出的灵魂,
还是轻敲我心扉想进来的尘世之魂呢?

168
That which oppresses me,
is it my soul trying to come out in the open,
or the soul of the world knocking at
my heart for its entrance?

169

思想以它独有的文字喂养自己,
成长茁壮。

170

我将我心之空瓶浸没在这沉默的时刻中,
它便汲满了爱。

169

Thought feeds itself with its own words and grows.

170

I have dipped the vessel of my heart into this silent hour;
it has filled with love.

171

无论你有工作,还是赋闲也好。

当你一说:"让我们做点事吧!"

麻烦便开始出现了。

172

向日葵羞于视不知名的花为同类。

太阳冉冉升起,向不知名的花微笑道:

"你好吗,我的宝贝?"

171

Either you have work or you have not.

When you have to say,"Let us do something,"

then begins mischief.

172

The sunflower blushed to own the nameless flower as her kin.

The sun rose and smiled on it, saying,

" Are you well, my darling? "

173

"是谁如命运般驱策我向前?"

"正是在我背后大步走着的自己啊。"

174

云儿将水注满河流的水杯,

自己却隐逸在远山中。

173

"Who drives me forward like fate?"

"The Myself striding on my back."

174

The clouds fill the water-cups of the river,

hiding themselves in the distant hills.

175

我一路走来,

水不断从罐中泼洒而出,

最后只剩下一点点可供家用。

175

I spill water from my water-jar as

I walk on my way.

Very little remains for my home.

176

盆中的水清晰可见；

海里的水却黑沉无比。

小道理可以用文字话语说明白，

而大道理唯有伟大的沉默可证。

176

The water in a vessel is sparkling;

the water in the sea is dark.

The small truth has words that are clear;

the great truth has great silence.

177
你的微笑,是你自己园里的花朵;
你的话语,是你自己山中的松涛;
但是你的心呀,
却似我们都熟知的平常女人。

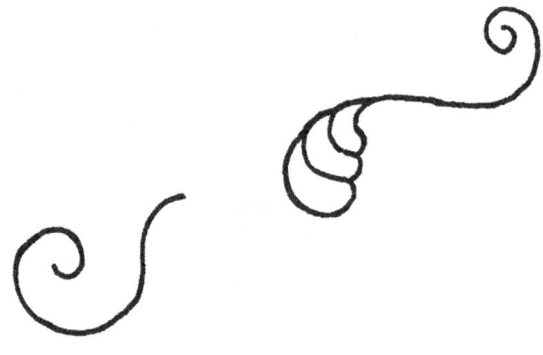

177
Your smile was the flowers of your own fields,
your talk was the rustle of your own mountain pines,
but your heart was the
woman that we all know.

178
我留给我爱的人,只是些小东西——
伟大事物全留给大家。

179
女人啊,
你用深深的泪水环绕着世界的心,
有如大海环绕着大地。

178

It is the little things that I leave behind for my loved ones,
—great things are for everyone.

179

Woman, thou hast encircled the world's heart with
the depth of thy tears as the sea has the earth.

180

阳光以微笑向我问候。

而雨,阳光忧伤的姊妹,向我心倾诉。

181

白昼的花落下花瓣,便被遗忘了。

此花入夜便成熟为记忆的金色果实。

180

The sunshine greets me with a smile.

The rain, his sad sister, talks to my heart.

181

My flower of the day dropped its petals forgotten.

In the evening it ripens into a golden fruit of memory.

182

我就像夜间小径，

在寂静中细听着记忆的足音。

183

薄暮天空对我来讲，

就像一扇窗，一盏点亮的灯，

以及那灯后的等待。

182
I am like the road in the night listening to the footfalls of its memories in silence.

183
The evening sky to me is like a window, and a lighted lamp, and a waiting behind it.

184
太急于行善的人，
反而找不到时间修身养性。

185
我是秋天的云，
空空无雨，
却在稻熟的田里看见我的圆满。

184
He who is too busy doing good finds no time to be good.

185
I am the autumn cloud, empty of rain,
see my fullness in the field of ripened rice.

186

他们愤世、杀戮，世人反竟称颂他们。
然而上帝却羞愧得急着将他的记忆埋藏在青草下。

187

脚趾乃是那些抛弃过去的手指。

186

They hated and killed and men praised them.
But God in shame hastens to
hide his memory under the green grass.

187

Toes are the fingers that have forsaken their past.

188

黑暗趋向光明,盲目则走向死亡。

189

受人们溺宠的小狗,
疑心宇宙密谋篡夺它的地位。

188

Darkness travels towards light,
but blindness towards death.

189

The pet dog suspects the universe for
scheming to take its place.

190

静静地坐着吧,我心,

毋须扬起你的尘土。

让世界自己寻着它的路找向你。

190

Sit still, my heart, do not raise your dust.

Let the world find its way to you.

191

弓对即将离弦的箭低语道：

"你的自由就是我的自由。"

192

女人啊，

你的笑声中，

蕴含生命之泉的乐章。

191

The bow whispers to the arrow before it speeds forth—

"Your freedom is mine."

192

Woman, in your laughter you have the
music of the fountain of life.

193

塞满理智的心,犹如一把全是锋刃的刀,
让用它的人伤手流血。

194

神喜爱人间的灯火,
尤胜于他自己伟大的星辰。

193

A mind all logic is like a knife all blade.
It makes the hand bleed that uses it.

194

God loves man's lamp lights better than
his own great stars.

195

这本是狂风暴雨的世界，

已被优美的音乐平服了。

196

晚霞向太阳说：

"我的心宛如收藏着您的吻的金色宝盒。"

195

This world is the world of wild storms kept tame with

the music of beauty.

196

"My heart is like the golden casket of thy kiss,"

said the sunset cloud to the sun.

197

近距离接触可能毁掉它,

保持距离或许能拥有它。

198

蟋蟀的唧唧声,雨的啪嗒声,

穿过黑暗传到我耳边,

仿佛是从我旧时青春梦传来的回响。

197

By touching you may kill,

by keeping away you may possess.

198

The cricket's chirp and the patter of rain

come to me through the dark,

like the rustle of dreams from my past youth.

199

"我失去了我的露珠。"

——花儿向星辰落尽的晨空这般哭嚷。

200

燃烧的木头迸出熊熊火花,

喊道:"这是我的花朵,我的死亡。"

199

"I have lost my dewdrop,"

cries the flower to the morning sky that has lost all its stars.

200

The burning log bursts in flame and cries,

—"This is my flower, my death."

201

黄蜂认为旁邻蜜蜂的蜂巢太小了。

蜜蜂却要他造一个更小的。

201

The wasp thinks that the honey-hive of

the neighbouring bees is too small.

His neighbours ask him to build one still smaller.

202

"我留不住你的浪花。"

河岸对河流说话。

"就让我将你的足迹留在我心里吧。"

203

白昼，以它小小地球的喧嚣，

淹没整个宇宙的沉静。

202

"I cannot keep your waves," says the bank to the river.

"Let me keep your footprints in my heart."

203

The day, with the noise of this little earth,

drowns the silence of all worlds.

204

歌声感到空气的无限,绘画感到大地的无限,

而诗,则感到空气与大地的无限;

因为诗的词义能舞动,诗的音韵能翱翔。

204

The song feels the infinite in the air,

the picture in the earth,

the poem in the air and the earth;

For its words have meaning that walks and music that soars.

205

当太阳西落,

清晨的东方已然悄立在他面前。

206

别让我有负于世界,

再拿它来对抗我。

205

When the sun goes down to the West,

the East of his morning stands before him in silence.

206

Let me not put myself wrongly to

my world and set it against me.

207

赞扬使我感到羞愧，

因为我其实偷偷地希求着它。

208

当我无事可做时，让我什么也不做，

安详地进入深深的平和中，

一如风平浪静的滨海暮色。

207

Praise shames me, for I secretly beg for it.

208

Let my doing nothing when I have nothing to do

become untroubled in its depth of

peace like the evening

in the seashore when the water is silent.

209

少女啊,你的纯真,

宛如湖水的蓝,展现出你的淳厚。

210

至善不独至,万物皆相随。

209

Maiden, your simplicity,

like the blueness of the lake,

reveals your depth of truth.

210

The best does not come alone.

It comes with the company of the all.

211

上帝的右手是仁慈的,

可怕的是他的左手。

(注:上帝的右手代表着恩典,左手则代表善恶的审判。)

212

我的夜晚从陌生的林中走来,

说着晨星听不懂的话语。

211

God's right hand is gentle,

but terrible is his left hand.

212

My evening came among the
alien trees and spoke in a language which
my morning stars did not know.

213

夜的黑像个袋子,

迸放出黎明的金色光芒。

214

我们的欲望将彩虹的颜色,

借给生命的烟雾。

213

Night's darkness is a bag that

bursts with the gold of the dawn.

214

Our desire lends the colours of

the rainbow to the mere mists and vapours of life.

215

神等着赢回自己的花朵,
将之当作是人类献给他的礼物收取。

216

我忧伤的思绪,
一直缠着我问他们自己的名字。

215

God waits to win back his own flowers
as gifts from man's hands.

216

My sad thoughts tease me asking me
their own names.

217
果实的奉献是珍贵的,
花儿的奉献是甜美的;
然而我只想做绿叶,
卑微地奉献一方绿荫。

217
The service of the fruit is precious,
the service of the flower is sweet,
but let my service be the service of
the leaves in its shade of humble devotion.

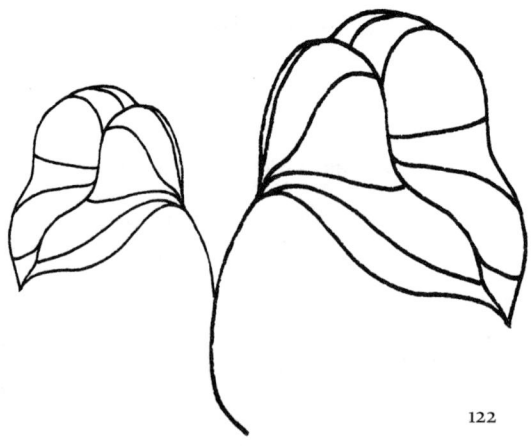

218

我的心扬起帆,

乘着慵懒的风,

驶向无所不在的奇幻岛。

219

群众是残暴的,

但人本身是善良的。

218

My heart has spread its sails to the idle winds for

the shadowy island of Anywhere.

219

Men are cruel, but Man is kind.

220

让我做您的杯子吧,

将我斟满的酒水献给您及您的人。

221

狂风暴雨就像某个被大地拒绝了爱的天神,

在痛苦中哭喊着。

220

Make me thy cup and let my fullness be for thee and for thine.

221

The storm is like the cry of some god in pain whose love the earth refuses.

222

世界不会因为死亡而流失，

毕竟死亡并不是一条裂痕。

223

生命因失去的

爱情而变得更丰富。

222

The world does not leak because death is not a crack.

223

Life has become richer

by the love that has been lost.

224

我的朋友,

你伟大的心随着东方旭日的光芒闪现,

好似黎明中的孤山雪峰。

225

死亡之泉,

教生命的止水再度流动。

224

My friend, your great heart shone with

the sunrise of the East like the snowy summit of

a lonely hill in the dawn.

225

The fountain of death makes the still water of life play.

226

那些拥有一切唯缺您的人,

我的上帝,

嘲笑着那些一无所有但只有您的人。

227

生命的跃动,

在它自己的音乐中得到了憩息。

226

Those who have everything but thee,

my God,

laugh at those who have nothing but thyself.

227

The movement of life has its rest in its own music.

228
踢脚只会扬起地上的尘土,
无法使土地长出禾米来。

229
我们的名字是夜浪中的闪闪波光,
不留任何痕迹便消逝了。

228
Kicks only raise dust and not crops from the earth.

229
Our names are the light that glows on the sea waves at night and then dies without leaving its signature.

230

让看得到玫瑰花的人,

只看到花的刺吧。

231

在鸟翼镶上黄金,

它便永远无法再翱翔于穹苍了。

230

Let him only see the thorns

who has eyes to see the rose.

231

Set the bird's wings with gold and

it will never again soar in the sky.

232
跟我们家乡一样的荷花,
在这片陌生水域绽开,
同样芬芳,只是换了个名字。

232
The same lotus of our clime blooms here in the
alien water with the same sweetness,
under another name.

233

以心透视，远方如临眼前。

234

月亮将她的光洒满天际，

黑点却留给自己。

233

In heart's perspective the distance looms large.

234

The moon has her light all over the sky,

her dark spots to herself.

235

别说:"这是清晨。"

接着便以"昨日"之名屏弃它。

将它视为初次见面、还未有名字的新生儿吧。

236

青烟向天空夸口,

灰烬则向大地吹嘘,

他们都宣称自己是火的兄弟。

235

Do not say,"It is morning,"

and dismiss it with a name of yesterday.

See it for the first time as a new-born child that has no name.

236

Smoke boasts to the sky,

and Ashes to the earth,

that they are brothers to the fire.

237

雨滴轻声向茉莉花说：

"请将我永远留在你心中。"

茉莉花叹了一声"唉"，便坠落在地了。

238

The raindrop whispered to the jasmine,

"Keep me in your heart for ever."

The jasmine sighed,"Alas,"

and dropped to the ground.

238

羞怯的思绪啊,请别怕我,
我是个诗人。

239

在我心幽微的沉默中,似乎充满蟋蟀的唧唧声——
有如声音的微弱暮色。

238

Timid thoughts, do not be afraid of me.
I am a poet.

239

The dim silence of my mind seems filled with crickets' chirp—
the grey twilight of sound.

240

火箭啊,你对星辰的侮辱,

又跟着你回到大地了。

241

您曾带领我走过白天拥挤的旅程,

进入我日暮孤寂中。

我在夜的寂静里,等待着它的意义显现。

240

Rockets,

your insult to the stars follows yourself

back to the earth.

241

Thou hast led me through my crowded travels of

the day to my evening's loneliness.

I wait for its meaning through the stillness of the night.

242

生命好比横渡海洋,

我们在同一艘狭小的船上相遇。

死亡时,你我便到岸了,

接着又各自奔向不同的世界。

242

This life is the crossing of a sea,

where we meet in the same narrow ship.

In death we reach the shore and go to our different worlds.

243

"真理"之河,

如常流过它"错误"的支流。

244

今天我的心想家了,

思念跨越时间之海重返那个甜蜜时刻。

243

The stream of truth flows through

its channels of mistakes.

244

My heart is homesick today for

the one sweet hour across the sea of time.

245

鸟鸣是曙光照在大地，
反射而来的回音。

246

晨光问金凤花：
"你是否骄傲得不肯吻我？"

245

The bird-song is the echo of
the morning light back from the earth.

246

"Are you too proud to kiss me?"
the morning light asks the buttercup.

247

"喔，太阳，我该如何对您歌唱、崇拜您呢？"

——小花问道。

"只要用你纯洁的全然静默。"

——太阳回道。

247

"How may I sing to thee and worship,

O Sun?"

asked the little flower.

"By the simple silence of thy purity,"

answered the sun.

248
当人类只是动物时，
比动物还不如。

249
乌云被光吻过后，
便成了天堂之花。

248
Man is worse than an animal
when he is an animal.

249
Dark clouds become heaven's flowers
when kissed by light.

250

莫让刀锋嘲笑刀柄的弩钝。

251

夜的寂静，

宛如一盏深幽的灯，燃烧着银河之光。

250

Let not the sword-blade mock

its handle for being blunt.

251

The night's silence,

like a deep lamp,

is burning with the light of its Milky Way.

252
生命犹如一座阳光岛屿，
大海日日夜夜在它周围，
唱着无尽的死亡之歌。

252
Around the sunny island of Life swells day and night death's limitless song of the sea.

253

这座山不就像一朵花,

透过它宛如花瓣的山丘,

畅享着阳光?

254

当真实的意义被曲解时,

便本末倒置,变成了"不真实"。

253

Is not this mountain like a flower,

with its petals of hills, drinking the sunlight?

254

The real with its meaning read wrong and

emphasis misplaced is the unreal.

255

我的心呀，

从世界的运转中去寻找你的美吧，

一如船拥有风与水的助力那般。

256

眼睛不以视力为傲，

却以所戴的眼镜自豪。

255

Find your beauty, my heart,

from the world's movement,

like the boat that has the grace of the wind and the water.

256

The eyes are not proud of

their sight but of their eyeglasses.

257
我住在自己的小小世界里，生怕这世界减少分毫。
把我带到您的世界吧，
让我拥有即使失去一切也能欣然接受的自由。

257
I live in this little world of
mine and am afraid to make it the least less.
Lift me into thy world
and let me have the freedom gladly to lose my all.

258

错误永远不可能因权力的增长而变成真理。

259

我的心，渴望随着歌声的音韵，

轻抚这阳光灿烂的绿色世界。

258

The false can never grow into truth

by growing in power.

259

My heart,

with its lapping waves of song,

longs to caress this green world of the sunny day.

260

路边的小草啊，爱那星辰吧，

你的梦想随即在花里实现。

261

让你的音乐化身一把利剑，

穿透尘世的喧嚣，直击中心吧。

260

Wayside grass, love the star,

then your dreams will come out in flowers.

261

Let your music, like a sword,

pierce the noise of the market to its heart.

262

这棵树颤抖的叶子,犹如婴孩的手指,

触动我心弦。

263

小花躺在尘土里,

寻找着蝴蝶飞过的路径。

262

The trembling leaves of this tree touch my heart

like the fingers of an infant child.

263

The little flower lies in the dust.

It sought the path of the butterfly.

264

我在歧路世界徘徊。

黑夜降临了,

请打开您的门吧,

通往您如家的世界那扇门。

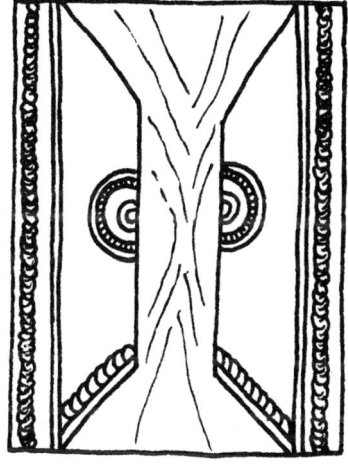

264

I am in the world of the roads.

The night comes.

Open thy gate,

thou world of the home.

265

我已唱过您白昼的歌。

夜晚时,让我拿着您的灯,

走过风雨飘摇的路吧。

265

I have sung the songs of thy day.

In the evening let me

carry thy lamp through the stormy path.

266

我不要求你进我屋里来。

请走进我无尽的孤寂吧,我的爱人。

267

死亡,与生一样,都属于生命的一部分。

举足,与落足一样,都是行走的一部分。

266

I do not ask thee into the house.

Come into my infinite loneliness, my Lover.

267

Death belongs to life as birth does.

The walk is in the raising of the foot as

in the laying of it down.

268

我已明了您同花儿与阳光低语的含义,

那很容易明白——

教我也明白您在痛苦与死亡中诉说的话语吧。

268

I have learnt the simple meaning of

thy whispers in flowers and sunshine—teach me to

know thy words in pain and death.

269

黑夜之花开迟了，当清晨亲吻她时，
她颤抖又叹息，接着便凋落在地。

270

透过万物的哀伤，
我听见大地之母的轻声哼唱。

269

The night's flower was late when
the morning kissed her,
she shivered and sighed and dropped to the ground.

270

Through the sadness of all things
I hear the crooning of the Eternal Mother.

271
大地啊,我以陌生人的身份来到你岸边,
以客人的身份住在你屋里,
今时则以朋友的身份走出你家门。

272
待我离去,让我的思想陪伴着你,
就像日落余晖,依傍在寂静星空的边缘。

271
I came to your shore as a stranger,
I lived in your house as a guest,
I leave your door as a friend,
my earth.

272
Let my thoughts come to you, when I am gone,
like the afterglow of sunset at the margin of starry silence.

273

在我心底点亮那颗晚安的星辰,

再让黑夜向我低诉爱吧。

274

我是迷失在暗夜中的孩子。

我从重重夜幕中向您伸出双手,母亲。

273

Light in my heart the evening star of rest and

then let the night whisper to me of love.

274

I am a child in the dark.

I stretch my hands through the coverlet of night for thee,

Mother.

275

一天的工作结束了,

让我将脸埋进您的臂弯吧,母亲。

让我坠入梦乡。

276

相聚时的灯光,不觉长明;

唯离别时,恍觉灭于一瞬。

275

The day of work is done. Hide my face in your arms, Mother.

Let me dream.

276

The lamp of meeting burns long;

it goes out in a moment at the parting.

277

喔,世界啊,当我死去时,

请在您的沉寂中替我留下一句话:

"我已然爱过。"

277

One word keep for me in thy silence,

O World,

when I am dead,

"I have loved."

278

当我们爱这个世界时,

才算真正活在这个世界上。

279

让死者享有不朽之名,

但让生者拥有不灭之爱。

278

We live in this world when we love it.

279

Let the dead have the immortality of fame,

but the living the immortality of love.

280

我曾见到您,

就像半睡半醒的孩子在黎明微光中看到母亲那样,

接着笑了笑,便又睡着了。

280

I have seen thee as the half-awakened child sees his mother in the dusk of the dawn and then smiles and sleeps again.

281

我将一次又一次死去,

好去明白生命的无穷无尽。

282

当我随拥挤的人潮走在路上时,

看见您从阳台上投过来的微笑,

引使我哼着歌,忘却一切烦嚣。

281

I shall die again and again to know that

life is inexhaustible.

282

While I was passing with the crowd in the road

I saw thy smile from the balcony and

I sang and forgot all noise.

283

爱是圆满的生命,

就像盛满了酒的酒杯。

284

他们在自己的庙里,

点燃自己的灯,吟唱着自己的歌。

但是鸟儿却在您的晨光里,

唱着您的名

——因为您的名便是喜乐。

283

Love is life in its fullness like

the cup with its wine.

284

They light their own lamps and

sing their own words in their temples.

But the birds sing thy

name in thine own morning light,

—for thy name is joy.

285
引领我到您沉静的中心,
好使我的心充满歌声。

286
就让他们活在自己所选的灿烂烟火世界中吧。
我的心只渴望您的星光呀,我的上帝。

285

Lead me in the centre of thy silence to

fill my heart with songs.

286

Let them live who choose in

their own hissing world of fireworks.

My heart longs for thy stars,

my God.

287
爱的痛苦围困着我的生命悲吟,
仿如深不可测的大海;
而爱的喜悦就像鸟儿在花丛中欢唱。

287
Love's pain sang round my life like
the unplumbed sea,
and love's joy sang like birds in
its flowering groves.

288

假如您想的话,就把灯捻熄了吧。

我将了解您的黑暗,也会爱着它。

288

Put out the lamp when thou wishest.

I shall know thy darkness and shall love it.

289

当白日将尽,我站在您面前时,

　　　　您将看见我的伤疤,

并明白我也有过创伤与业已愈合的伤口。

289

When I stand before thee at the day's end

thou shalt see my scars and know that

I had my wounds and also my healing.

290

总有一天,

我会在另一个世界的旭日下对您歌唱:

"我曾在地球的光里,在人类的爱里,见过您。"

290

Some day I shall sing to thee in the

sunrise of some other world,

"I have seen thee before in the light of the earth,

in the love of man."

291

往日的浮云飘进我的生命里，

不再滴雨或兴起风暴，

只是为我日夕穹空添上一抹彩霞。

291

Clouds come floating into my life from

other days no longer to shed rain or usher storm

but to give colour to my sunset sky.

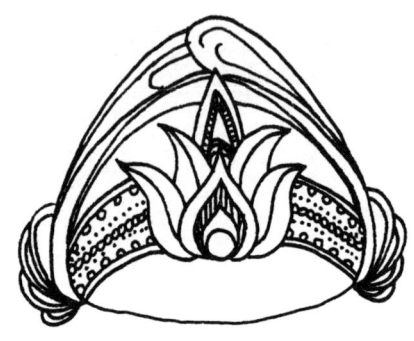

292

真理激起对抗它的风暴,

风暴反将真理的种子散播开来。

293

昨夜的风暴,

为今日晓晨戴上了金色的宁和之冠。

292

Truth raises against itself the storm that scatters its seeds broadcast.

293

The storm of the last night has crowned this morning with golden peace.

294

真理似乎总在它最后的话语中显现；
而这最后的话语又衍生出下一个真理。

295

他是有福之人，
因其外在名声的光环未掩盖过他的真实。

294

Truth seems to come with its final word;
and the final word gives birth to its next.

295

Blessed is he whose fame does not outshine his truth.

296

当我忘记自己的名时,
您名字的甜美总充满我心——
宛如蒙雾消失后的晨曦。

297

静谧的黑夜有着母亲的美,
喧闹的白昼则有孩子的美。

296

Sweetness of thy name fills my heart when
I forget mine—like thy morning sun
when the mist is melted.

297

The silent night has the beauty of the mother
and the clamorous day of the child.

298

人微笑时,世界爱他;
人大笑时,世界便怕他了。

299

神静待世人在智慧中重拾童年。

298

The world loved man when he smiled.
The world became afraid of him when he laughed.

299

God waits for man to
regain his childhood in wisdom.

300
让我感知这世界是您爱的体现，
那么我也将用爱来帮助这世界。

301
您的阳光对我心里的寒冬绽出微笑，
从不怀疑它也有春日花朵。

300
Let me feel this world as thy love taking form,
then my love will help it.

301
Thy sunshine smiles upon the winter days of my heart,
never doubting of its spring flowers.

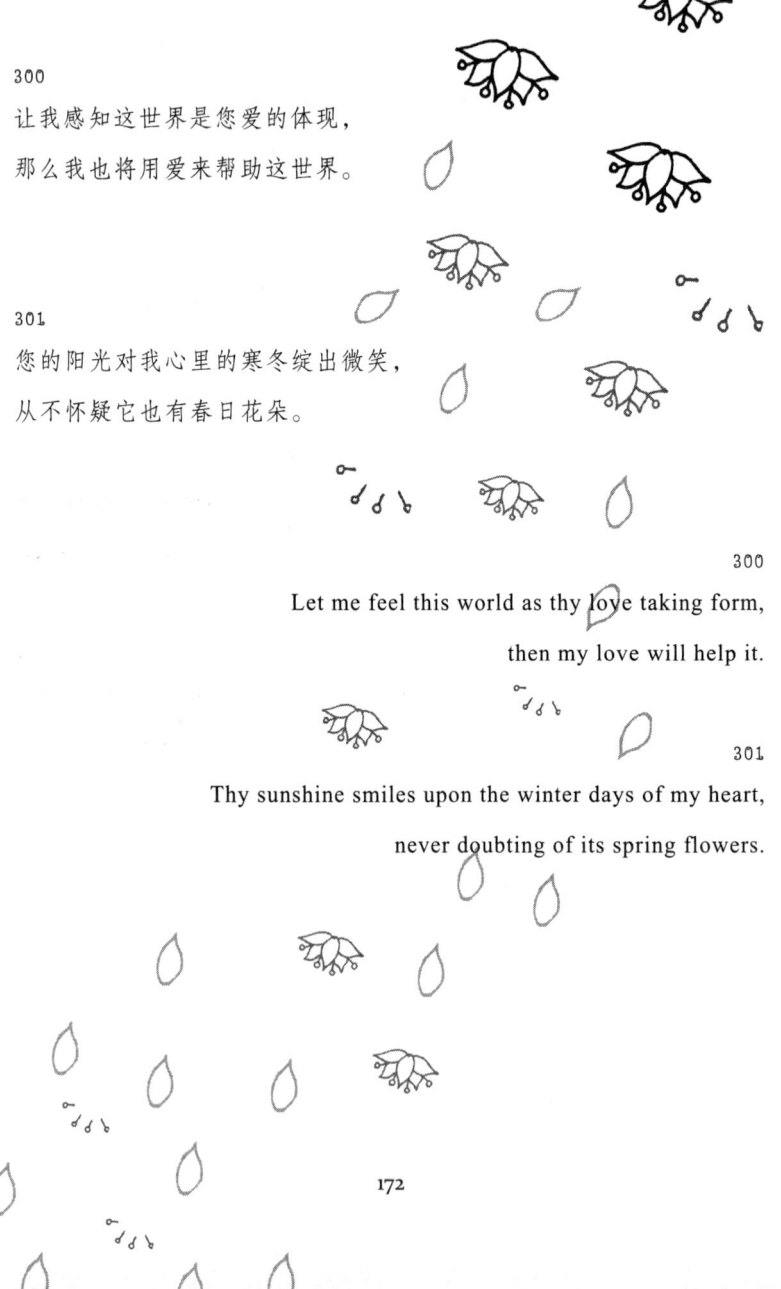

302

神在爱中亲吻世人之"有限",

而人则亲吻神之"无限"。

303

您穿越荒芜岁月中无数的漠地,

终抵圆满的那一刻。

302

God kisses the finite in

His love and man the infinite.

303

Thou crossest desert lands of barren years.

304

神的静默，

使人的思想成熟为语言。

305

永恒的旅人呀，

您将在我的歌声中，觅得您留下的足迹。

304

God's silence ripens man's thoughts into speech.

305

Thou wilt find, Eternal Traveller,

marks of thy footsteps across my songs.

306

父亲,

将您的光辉展现在您的孩子身上,

让我不致使您蒙羞。

306

Let me not shame thee,

Father,

who displayest thy glory in thy children.

307

这是个惨淡无趣的日子,

乌云下的光,就像被处罚的孩子,

苍白的脸上挂着泪痕;

而风的咆哮,仿如受伤世界的哭嚎声。

但是我知道,

自己正踏在会见挚友的路上。

307

Cheerless is the day,

the light under frowning clouds is

like a punished child with traces of tears on its pale cheeks,

and the cry of the wind is like the cry of a wounded world.

But I know I am travelling to meet my Friend.

308

今晚，棕榈叶生起一阵骚动，

　　　海面忽起一阵汹涌，

满月，就像世界之心的悸动。

　　　您从哪个未知的天空，

　　默默捎来爱的痛苦秘密？

308

Tonight there is a stir among the palm leaves,

a swell in the sea,

Full Moon, like the heart-throb of the world.

From what unknown sky hast thou carried in

thy silence the aching secret of love?

309
我梦见一颗星,那是座光明之岛,
我将在那里出生;
在那充满活力又深幽无扰之地,
我的生命将完成它的使命,
就像秋阳下的稻田。

309
I dream of a star, an island of light,
where I shall be born and in the depth of
its quickening leisure my life will ripen
its works like the rice-field in the autumn sun.

310

雨中湿土的气息,
宛如由一群沉默平民大众口中合唱出的伟大颂歌。

311

"爱情也可能会失去",
乃是我们无法将之视为真理接受的事实。

310

The smell of the wet earth in the
rain rises like a great chant of praise from
the voiceless multitude of the insignificant.

311

That love can ever lose is a fact that
we cannot accept as truth.

312

总有一天我们会明白,
死亡永远夺不走我们心灵获得的东西——
因为心灵获得的东西已与她结成一体。

312

We shall know some day that

death can never rob us of that which our soul has gained,

for her gains are one with herself.

313

神在属于我的黄昏暮色中，

带着我过去的花朵来到这儿，

而这些花儿在他的篮子中，依然保持鲜丽。

313

God comes to me in the dusk

of my evening with the flowers from my past kept fresh

in His basket.

314

主啊，当我将生命之弦都调好音后，

您的每一次触动，便会奏出爱的乐音。

315

我的主啊，让我真实地活着吧，

这么一来，死亡对我也会变得真实。

314

When all the strings of my life will be tuned,

my Master,

then at every touch of thine will come out the music of love.

315

Let me live truly,

my Lord,

so that death to me become true.

316

人类的历史,

耐心地等候着受辱者胜利那一天。

317

我感觉到此刻您正凝视着我的心,

犹如清晨沉静的旭光,

洒落在收成后的寂寥田野上。

316

Man's history is waiting in patience for

the triumph of the insulted man.

317

I feel thy gaze upon my heart this moment like

the sunny silence of the morning upon

the lonely field whose harvest is over.

318

我渴望渡过这汹涌的"咆哮之海",

抵达"歌之岛"。

319

夜以落日之音揭开序曲,

对其无以言喻的黑暗,

吟唱着神圣颂歌。

318

I long for the Island of Songs across
this heaving Sea of Shouts.

319

The prelude of the night is commenced
in the music of the sunset,
in its solemn hymn to the ineffable dark.

320

我曾登上高峰,
发现大名鼎鼎的贫脊荒芜高处,
毫无遮蔽之地。
我的向导呀,在光消逝之前,
引领我到宁静的山谷吧!
在那儿,
生命的收获将熟成为金黄色的智慧。

320

I have scaled the peak and found no shelter in
fame's bleak and barren height.
Lead me, my Guide,
before the light fades,
into the valley of quiet where life's harvest mellows into
golden wisdom.

321
在薄暮的灰朦中，
一切事物都显得如此诡谲——
尖塔的底层消失于黑暗中，
树梢宛如斑斑墨渍。
我将等待清晨醒来时，
睹见您光明中的城市。

321
Things look phantastic in this dimness of
the dusk—the spires whose bases are lost
in the dark and tree-tops like blots of ink.
I shall wait for the morning and wake up
to see thy city in the light.

322

我曾经历过苦难及绝望,

亦曾体见过死亡,

而今何其欣喜自己活在这伟大的世界中。

322

I have suffered and despaired and
known death and I am glad that
I am in this great world.

323

在我的生命中,

有些荒凉寂静的地带。

那是我忙碌的日子里,

汲取阳光与空气的开阔之处。

324

让我从不圆满的过去中解脱吧!

过去的种种,从身后紧紧纠缠着我,

让死亡也变得困难。

323

There are tracts in my life that are bare and silent.

They are the open spaces

where my busy days had their light and air.

324

Release me from my unfulfilled past clinging to

me from behind making death difficult.

325

就以这句话作为我的结语吧：

"我信您的爱。"

325

Let this be my last word,

that I trust in thy love.